The Blog

Bad Time for Poetry

ARTISTS AND WRITERS SERIES

The Blog

Bad Time for Poetry

August 24, 2007 – May 25, 2009

Enrique Martínez Celaya

PARA CARLOS Y FERNANDO
En gratitud por su compañia en este viaje

CONTENTS

The Blog

Bad Time for Poetry

August 24, 2007 – May 25, 2009

The First Entry

Friday, August 24, 2007

The name of this blog is from Brecht.

Anderson Ranch Reading List

Saturday, August 25, 2007

I am enclosing a starter list of books on art and ideas that I consider useful to have read. Don't look for a common point of view, as it is not here; this list does not "add up."

Art After Modernism by Brian Wallis
The Genius Decision by K. Ottmann
Camera Lucida by Roland Barthes
The Anti-Aesthetic by Hal Foster
Less than One by Joseph Brodsky
The Shape of Content by Ben Shahn
Nietzsche's Philosophy of Art by J. Young
Culture and Value by L. Wittgenstein
Selected Essays by John Berger
Painting as an Art by Richard Wollheim

Adorno as Cliché

Sunday, August 26, 2007

The frequent reference to Adorno's pronouncement, "to write a poem after Auschwitz is barbaric,"[1] is problematic for at least four reasons:

1. The phrase is customarily presented outside of the context in which it appeared: "The critique of culture is confronted with the last stage in the dialectic of culture and barbarism: to write a poem after Auschwitz is barbaric, and that corrodes also the knowledge which expresses why it has become impossible to write poetry today."

2. The reference frequently comes with—particularly in academic contexts—a pompous undercurrent, as if seeking "ahhh" as a follow up.

3. It is rarely acknowledged that Adorno reconsidered his words: "Perennial suffering has as much right to expression as the tortured have to scream... hence it may have been wrong to say that no poem could be written after Auschwitz."

4. If Auschwitz invalidates anything it is poetry whose nature or quality does not measure up. Auschwitz didn't draw a line on the landscape of art that was not already there.

Intellectual Affectations

Wednesday, August 29, 2007

Today a press release arrived via email. Here it is:

In his first solo exhibition at the Fredric Snitzer Gallery, Timothy Buwalda presents ambitious, large scale paintings, and several mono-prints that investigate the theme of hope in the negative; or, to take it a step further, hope in negation. They are reminiscent of what Richard Diebenkorn wrote in *Notes to Myself on Beginning a Painting*: "Mistakes can't be erased but they move you from your present position."

Buwalda uses wrecked cars as a metaphor for potential being squandered or not realized, but is ironically hopeful and quiet. The images weave back and forth between photorealism and abstraction. The use of various painting techniques within the same painting points to a search of painting language and the exploration of its limitations (this too at times explores negation).

Buwalda writes, "These paintings arrived from two distinct places for me. Firstly, reflection of my own life and how there are these 'check points' you are supposed to arrive at by certain time constraints (what do you do if you miss these?). Secondly, the process of paint itself. I feel these things overlap along the way, that there is a parallel between the process of painting and life, how you have to work with the negative, oftentimes, to get somewhere further than your original vision."

7

The exhibition will be on view at the Fredric Snitzer Gallery 2247 NW 1st PL Miami, FL 33127. Hours are 10am to 5pm Tuesday through Saturday. There will be an opening reception held on Saturday, September 8th, from 7:30 - 10 pm.

For some time now people have been exploiting the potential of art and its discourse as signs of intellectual prowess. In my experience of the contemporary art world, the desire to be brilliant trumps most other whims and vanities.

In this brief entry I will not explore why this might be the case. Instead, I will suggest that there are better ways to give the impression of intellectual rigor than this press release. It should be apparent that, even if poorly executed, a strategy is at play here: the press release could have mentioned Robert Bechtle or Charles Ray instead of the somewhat puzzling Diebenkorn reference (that R.D. is sharing space with the claims in this press release shows no one is safe in the art world), or the emphasis could have been on the choice of subject matter or on another topic that the artist and his representatives actually understood. But instead they chose to write of negation, painting language and its limitations hoping to decorate what is obviously fairly thin content with the afterglow of Saussure, Baudrillard, et.al.

This gesture is, unfortunately, commonplace—it is a strategy of choice.

Intellectual ornament is popular because it only demands minor understanding of the ideas at play (perhaps as little as just the names) and it works because it only requires recognition, not understanding, from its audience. It relies on fast reads in the hope of getting away with statements like, "The use of various painting techniques within the same painting points to a search of painting language and the exploration of its limitations (this too at times explores negation)."

The "hard thinking" which has been de rigueur in the last forty years (just to pick a time) is at best amusing and at worst pathetic. Wasted time. I wonder how much could be done by Timothy Buwalda if he were to actually consider and work within the complexity of painting, without the tiresome escape of theories he has heard mentioned. Authentic engagement might show him, as it shows us all, that it is easier to hit against one's limitations than those of painting.

The End of the Day in Florida

Wednesday, August 29, 2007

On my way to the 7-Eleven (a trip I take a few times a day), I walked through the empty studio courtyard. The amber-colored light was falling on the hibiscus and the silver-button bushes; the air was warm, had some salt in it and it smelled, as it often does, of soap thanks to the laundromat three buildings away.

Late afternoons in Florida have the stillness and glow of de Chirico paintings, except here the sky has more range. Since I am leaving soon, I stopped to notice it, and while looking around at the palm trees and sandy soil, I wondered why I paint winter landscapes.

I wasn't there long when the repair shop next door, which usually closes early, began grinding something. It was annoying at first but then it helped settle some sort of order, an order in which the winter paintings didn't seem as odd. However, it was not a relief.

The Road

Saturday, September 1, 2007

Bolle, the main character of Harry Martinson's *The Road*, wanders through the Swedish countryside. Here is one passage:

> So I went, and all that summer I tramped round the country, heard the birds sing, bathed in quiet streams and lakes and roamed through glens and valleys where the grass was dewy and clean. Clouds drifted, winds moved in the woods, flowers bowed and gleamed, bumble-bees buzzed in the clover, girls sang in the hay-fields.[2]

Bolle's aim is the wandering itself. It is a lifestyle for which he pays in fear and detachment, but for him it is a worthwhile trade: as a tramp, he gains nature, he resists the externally imposed and he finds hope in what might be around the next turn of the road.

Many times I have fancied myself a Bolle, someone who chooses the road however unknown. But it is a fancy. Like Ungaretti, I am always ready for departures but, unlike Bolle, it is "ready" as in "expectant" nor as in "prepared."

Maybe no one can be prepared and maybe the road is not so much a choice. Maybe it is a reaction, which sometimes ends well and sometimes does not. When does it end well? Maybe as often as the settled life ends well, which is not often. But probably not even that much. What the road opens (irreversibly) is more sensible to keep close.

Martinson's book points at the limitations on freedom imposed by social arrangements, the oppression of machines and the tyranny of those who hand down the rules, but it makes less of an issue of the challenge posed by the past. Maybe his approach was to tackle an idea akin to "practical freedom," but it seems to me that the most intriguing questions come in search of "pure freedom," even if such a concept proves silly upon further analysis—and it does, I think.

Every event, good or bad, narrows what's possible and enslaves us in ways we often don't want to give up; ways the road won't always release. I have events, Bolle had events and Martinson as well; Martinson, the beautiful tramp, was ultimately disheartened by his.

And yet, who, at least sometimes, wouldn't want to wander or perhaps, to walk a mile without hypocrisy, without attachments?

The Road is too simple; one reason why it is touching.

The end is important in all things (I)

Tuesday, September 4, 2007

Nomad is almost finished and, as if to emphasize this finality, it has rained all afternoon. From time to time the sky looked like the sky in the summer painting.

The end is important in all things (II)

Wednesday, September 5, 2007

The ending of a body of work is like coming to the end of a good but difficult book: I wish I could stay in the world created by the work but the work itself expels me.

At the end of a series or a cycle there are no victorious trumpets and no certainty, at least for me. If a trumpet were to be heard it would be a little one, made of plastic, with a strident ironic sound. Instead of the sounds of victory, the ending of a series brings the confetti of doubt and regrets, questions about the works in the world, and ambivalence about parting with things I wish to keep.

Criticism and Imitation

Thursday, September 6, 2007

It is interesting to consider *Art's Prospect: the challenge of tradition in an age of celebrity* by Roger Kimball[3] in relation to *Stranger Shores: literary essays, 1986-1999* by J.M. Coetzee.[4] While quite different—and their difference is what I would like to highlight here—there are reasons to place them together for a moment: they are both non-aligned with the contemporary discourse—this is less true of Coetzee; both share a certain impatience with mediocrity; both writers have a considerable following; and they both feel it is reasonable to pass judgments on the work of others.

It is instructive to compare how they construct those judgments.

Roger Kimball usually makes his arguments by concatenating colorful sentences which are not always constrained by logic and that often sacrifice accuracy for energy. Here are two representative examples:

> A quick glance around our culture shows that the avant-garde assault on tradition has long since degenerated into a sclerotic orthodoxy. What established taste makers now herald as cutting-edge turns out time and again to be a stale reminder of past impotence.

It is a good rule of thumb in the contemporary art world that the level of pretension is inversely proportional to the level of artistic achievement.[5]

Roger Kimball is annoyed with the art world and his writings convey his annoyance through a writing style that is both ironic and bombastic. He has an extensive group of people and institutions he dislikes, and he also has a pantheon of artists he admires. The shared qualities of the former are easy to recognize—their cult of novelty, their "semi-beatified status," their "unbearable pretentiousness"—but the latter, the pantheon, does not seem to respond to a unified philosophy, instead Kimball would most likely say they share "quality."

What I find remarkable about Roger Kimball's writing is how thin it is. Once the exaggerated adjectives, the insults, the condescension and the many occurrences of "undoubtedly" and "it is clear," are removed there is very little left; and what's leftover is neither interesting nor new. This scarcity of substance is surprising considering Kimball stands for quality and lack of artifice above novelty and pretentiousness.

While I share much of Roger Kimball's dislike for the art world, I find *Art's Prospect* to be a weak argument in favor of or against anything. J.M. Coetzee's *Stranger Shores*, on the other hand, is an impressive example of what is possible when seriousness, quality and originality of thought combine.

The best case against the pretentious obscurity of Rosalind Krauss's writing is not Kimball's essay "Feeling Sorry for Rosalind Krauss" but the lucidity and intelligence of Coetzee's writings. Unlike Krauss or Kimball, Coetzee downplays rather than exaggerates his intellectuality, and his judgments on the work of others seem carefully assessed and measured in his effort to not be petty or arrogant. Coetzee's writing has a distinct voice without the need for the decorative flair and it comes across as profoundly knowledgeable without pedantic poses or fancy terminology.

Although other claims are voiced, we like to imitate and in an environment like art and academia, imitating intellectual stars (who Kimball is not but Coetzee and Krauss are) has significant rewards. It is easy to figure out how to write and think like Kimball. The reason we don't read more Kimball-like writings is because the people who write like him are usually standing on soapboxes not, unlike him, editing intellectual journals. It is also easy to figure out, but harder to execute, how to write and think like Krauss, and since the Krauss-type writings fit well within the vehicles of intellectual dissemination, we often read thinkers like Krauss—for instance, in the magazine *October*, which Krauss helped found. Coetzee is a different story. It is easy to see how he writes and thinks but he is very difficult to imitate because at the heart of his writing there is formidable intelligence, erudition and strength of character. I expect more Coetzee imitators to continue to appear but unlike the case of Krauss or Kimball, the Coetzee imitators are easy to distinguish from the original.

The end is important in all things (III)

Friday, September 7, 2007

From the Hagakure:

In the Kamigata area they have a sort of tiered lunch box they use for a single day when flower viewing. Upon returning, they throw them away, trampling them underfoot. As might be expected, this is one of my recollections of the capital [Kyoto]. The end is important in all things.[6]

A New Body of Work

Saturday, September 8, 2007

My project, *For two Martinson poems, poorly understood*, is now finished. It consists of paintings, sculptures and one photograph. It will be shown (it opens October 4th) at the John Berggruen Gallery in San Francisco.

In this series, like in most of the work of the past four or five years, I tried to explore (by tapping, maybe like a physician testing reflexes) the limits to holding basic questions of existence in thought or words or art; in particular, how those limits impose themselves on my efforts to consider new choices against a growing body of past choices. The concern here is not memory, as it has often been said about my work, but the past as a definite force on the present—as a comparative weight on the balance scale of meaning.

In this exploration of or inquiry about highly abstract ideas, I have used the poetry of the Russian Osip Mandelstam and the Swede Harry Martinson, both of whom, in deceivingly simple poems, transverse a lonely landscape of "the personal" while striving towards large and unwieldy concepts.

The imagery of this new body of work is dominated by trees, snow, horizon, light, soil and figures: I have pared down the work to those elements I consider fundamental in order to manifest and understand (better but, of course, poorly) the nature of choice, regrets and possibility. As always, this work is not the result of an a priori agenda of representational painting nor of a conceptual strategy. Instead, it is the CURRENT embodiment of my efforts towards making sense of the world as I want to make sense of it TODAY; tomorrow, I might work with words or empty rooms.

Neither culture (in the way "culture" is used in art writings) nor contemporary art have been considerations in this new body of work. If I had to locate this work anywhere outside of itself, it would be with poetry, but poetry in its most limited use of the framework created by Mandelstam and Martinson. To be more specific, not in any way involved with the "discourse of poetry" nor with "the poetic," a term frequently used to describe affected works lacking in strength of character.

Art and Embarrassment

Tuesday, September 11, 2007

Today I received the following announcement regarding the Lyon Biennial of Contemporary Art (don't laugh for too long: there's something not so funny hiding underneath the foolery):

2007 Lyon Biennial of Contemporary Art

00s - The history of a decade that has not yet been named

September 19, 2007 - January 6, 2008

Artistic direction : Thierry Raspail
Conception : Stéphanie Moisdon & Hans Ulrich Obrist
Production Management : Thierry Prat
Visual Identity : M/M (Paris)

Membres du jury:
Présidente Susanne Pagé, directrice de la Fondation Louis Vuitton pour la création, Paris
Gunnar Kvaran, directeur du Astrup Fearnley Museum of Modern Art, Oslo
Knight Landesman, Artforum
Samuel Keller, Art Basel
Elaine Sturtevant, artiste
Kasper König, Sculpture Project, Münster
Silvia Karman Cubina, The Moore Space, Miami

Preview : September 17-18, 2007
Opening : September 18, 2007

Conceived of as a history and geography manual in the form of a game, the 2007 Lyon Biennial is inviting sixty-six Players from all over the world, distributed in two circles. Forty-nine of them (curators, art critics...) are being asked to answer the following question: "Who, in your opinion, is the artist who best represents this decade?" A second circle is composed of nineteen other Players—mostly artists—each devising a program, a system or a problematics intended to define the decade in progress.

In Favor of Speaking Up

Wednesday, September 12, 2007

A friend sent me a note. It said that while he agreed with the comments about Rosalind Krauss, he was not sure of the value of such comments. And knowing him, a remarkable person, I think I understand where he is coming from. It is difficult to walk lightly through life when one is attacking, criticizing and the like. It increases one's burden—one's footprint. Moreover, what has been said is difficult to take back and difficult to forget. Instead of attacking or criticizing other people's views, the focus could be in living one's beliefs. In this way, it might be possible to remain light and unmarked by the stain of public words. It seems a more elegant way to live and it would be hard to argue against its rewards. In my book *Guide*, Thomas Hoveling lived like that.

I frequently consider the question, and while I am never completely comfortable with my actions, I have, so far, concluded that it is important to speak up. It is important to take a visible stand against ideas one judges incorrect, misleading or evil. It is a burden, an annoyance, one is frequently wrong, and speaking up is often a detour from other projects. But unless alternatives are heard or read, they almost don't exist, and ideas that don't exist are never re-discovered.

The Romantic (in the conventional use of the term) notion that greatness ultimately triumphs is the outcome of self-serving excuses and feel-good notions about life's fairness, and it is frequently justified with misunderstandings about history and misquoted biographies.

Ideas do not exist in isolation. They are refined and clarified through exchange. Weaknesses in one's position, for instance, are revealed quickly in the friction of a critique. It is easy to be pedantic about the value of one's ideas when those ideas are not tested, poked—used beyond their circle of safety. Silence, something I revere, is at certain times the greatest arrogance, and has been at some key moments the greatest immorality. Moreover, many of the keepers-to-themselves are disingenuous: they feel above struggle but harbor resentment, pride and self-importance.

There is also the issue of offering alternatives, particularly in the art world, which for all its "diversity" often appears (particularly to emerging artists and students) polarized as a whole and monolithic in the particular sub-space of the relevant mainstream. If you consider the art world from their point of view, it would seem a conglomerate of sectors defined by the *Artforum* crowd or by the neo-conservatives or by the gut-trusters or by one of the many other "interest groups." All these sectors have their canon, their loudspeakers, their publications.

So, if one believes something better or more authentic is possible, that belief should be shared and supported publicly. Many artists whose potential had not yet unfolded don't know what to think because they are bombarded everyday with, or intimidated by, ideas they distrust but don't know why. In our age there is a tendency towards polarization and tidy worldviews, so it is important to combat this tendency by putting "out there" the view that contradictions or dissonant points of view can co-exist in one mind, which makes me think of Fitzgerald: "The test of a first rate intelligence is the ability to hold two opposed ideas in the mind at the same time, and still retain the ability to function." So, one good reason to speak up is to put forth ideas and attitudes that are ambitious and honest enough to retain internal conflicts, conflicts whose resolution propels investigation and inquiry.

House Where Nobody Lives

Thursday, September 13, 2007

Our house is almost empty. The toys are gone and my family is gone. Only I am left behind—to finish a few projects. I did a walkthrough last night. It reminded me of that song by Tom Waits, "House Where Nobody Lives."

Complexity and Tidy Packages

Sunday, September 16, 2007

One can appreciate the complexity of a notion and work within that complexity, or one can try to simplify it to fit into a tidy package. Both ways have their merits but, usually, only the former advances the notion in ways that can be called something other than trivial. Why then pursue the "tidy package"? There are many motivations but I think most of them focus on the immediacy of certain rewards: tidy packages are portable, allowing application in a wide variety of situations; they usually don't require intense engagement; and they are frequently all that is required to advance socially and professionally (not only do tidy packages foster advances because they are sufficient to quench most people's thirst for knowledge and truth, but also because deeper engagements are usually not welcomed).

A while back I was at a gallery with a well-known collector who considers himself quite sharp. He stopped in front of one of Sol LeWitt's numbered pictograms. He leaned into the work. He squinted and tightened his lips, as if he was in thought. After a while he turned to me with something like insight in his eyes, and he spoke of the mathematical and conceptual power of the sets of numbers arranged in boxes. I told him I didn't see it and he looked at me with contempt. What serious mathematics could there be in those drawings, really? I don't know anyone, other than "art people," who goes to LeWitt's work in order to get structural or mathematical insight. It is math-lite, in the same way that some art works are politics-lite and and so on.

Remarkably (remarkably considering what one sees and reads) few people would admit to be interested in tidy packages.

The Times They Are a-Changin'

Sunday, September 16, 2007

Now I have finished *Nomad* which will be shown at the Miami Art Museum this fall and winter (opens to the public November 2). For better or for worse, the environment—its parts and their relationship—represents most of what I know about painting.

Earlier this afternoon, after I finished my notes on *Nomad* I went for a long swim in the ocean. The beach was empty. Then a skinny and hairy man sat down on the sand and turned on his radio. I got out of the water. We both nodded—he seemed homeless and his radio was small. I sat near my things and we both looked straight ahead, towards the horizon: a band of dark ocean under an almost white sky. I could hear his songs. They seemed to be coming from farther away than the twenty yards between us. Dylan's "The Times They Are a-Changin'" came on. While listening, I noticed the dark clouds moving above. I knew it wasn't going to rain but I left when the song ended, just in case.

Come gather 'round people
Wherever you roam
And admit that the waters
Around you have grown

And accept it that soon
You'll be drenched to the bone.
If your time to you
Is worth savin'
Then you better start swimmin'
Or you'll sink like a stone
For the times they are a-changin'.

Come writers and critics
Who prophesize with your pen
And keep your eyes wide
The chance won't come again
And don't speak too soon
For the wheel's still in spin
And there's no tellin' who
That it's namin'.
For the loser now
Will be later to win
For the times they are a-changin'.

Come senators, congressmen
Please heed the call
Don't stand in the doorway
Don't block up the hall
For he that gets hurt
Will be he who has stalled
There's a battle outside
And it is ragin'.
It'll soon shake your windows
And rattle your walls
For the times they are a-changin'.

Come mothers and fathers
Throughout the land
And don't criticize
What you can't understand
Your sons and your daughters
Are beyond your command
Your old road is
Rapidly agin'.
Please get out of the new one
If you can't lend your hand
For the times they are a-changin'.

The line it is drawn
The curse it is cast
The slow one now
Will later be fast
As the present now
Will later be past
The order is
Rapidly fadin'.
And the first one now
Will later be last
For the times they are a-changin'.

Art in South Florida

Tuesday, September 18, 2007

I think about Florida more consciously now that I am leaving and in particular, I think of the arts in South Florida.

First, there is the Florida landscape, the water that is everywhere and the changing sky: these are good points of reference for artists. The housing developments and malls notwithstanding, there is also an end-of-the-world-everything-could-happen-here sense to Florida that is freeing for artists trying to find themselves (which ought to mean all artists).

Miami is an international city in ways New York and Los Angeles are not. Surely, NY and LA have people from many nationalities but these groups are frequently relegated to ghettoes and parades, and their appearance on TV and newspapers is usually as victims or perpetrators of crimes. In South Florida minorities and people from other countries are a visible force, not just token exceptions, and since they represent a wide variety of nationalities and economic backgrounds, their causes, unlike in other places, tend to be more than just self-serving.

Another interesting and useful quality of the arts in South Florida is that here—with exceptions—people in the arts are a little insecure about their worth. Insecurity is good in the arts. It promotes self-discovery and expansion. This searching impetus can be of significance now that the Basel Fair and the proposed new Miami Art Museum are giving the arts in this region a boost. I think MAM has better leadership, scholarship and honesty than many museums—if this is not more obvious it is because they are relatively understated; hopefully the new building will bring the necessary attention to the museum.

But in order to develop a world-class art community, South Florida needs to overcome some challenges. For instance, Basel has been good for the city but furthering the art's community dependency on the Basel Fair is a precarious formula for success. Another danger is that the city can give in to the temptation of being a satellite of New York or a playground for the city's well-known collectors—there are already signs of some of this going on. An approach the city could take to develop itself independently of Basel, New York and powerful figures, is to encourage education and exhibition spaces. By education I mean rigorous art programs whose intellectual preoccupations go beyond reading art magazines and theory blurbs. By exhibition spaces I mean venues that range from the true alternative spaces to a lively gallery scene, which should include a few dealers concerned with art.

I am cautiously hopeful.

Reflections on a Return

Thursday, September 27, 2007

It has been five days since I left Florida. I am now in Los Angeles as if I had never left and in other ways, as if I had never lived here. Undoubtedly, my mindset is different, though I don't know how or if it will affect the work. From a distance, and without whatever clarity time might bring, Florida seems an important period. It might not be inaccurate to think of it as a self-imposed exile, thought I have to smirk at the idea of exiling oneself to anyplace in which there is a mall and a beach. But it was precisely that resort-quality of the little town in which I lived that wiped away the romantic aspirations to self-discovery and "toughness" that inevitably come up in pilgrimages to deserts, to Alaska or to New York. The charm of a little beach town, the homes decorated with coral, the gentle nights and the Lily Pulitzer outfits, meant that whatever ideas I wrestled had to be my own and, frequently, foreign to the day to day conditions. In other words, the angst of the artist in the little beach town is felt in sharp contrast to its surroundings. There is no nasty grit of the city or garbage or frostbite, no traditionally-grand landscape or historical weight to echo the brutality of living or to applaud the act of getting up in the morning.

Books for the Artist

Tuesday, October 9, 2007

Book suggestions are a frequent request. It would be useful—and probably more interesting—if these requests were included in the comments.

For now, a brief but useful list of books for the artist,

The Power of the Center by R. Arnheim
The Germans and Their Art: a troublesome relationship
  by H. Belting
Art as Experience by J. Dewey
The Epic of Gilgamesh

Nebraska Reading List

Friday, October 26, 2007

The following is a starter list of readings that might useful to the University of Nebraska MFA students. It is by no means complete. In addition, for those so inclined, I would suggest some introductory readings on Schopenhauer and Kierkegaard, because they have had a significant impact on art and literature, also John Dewey's "Art as Experience," which I suggested in an earlier reading list. For those of you with a sense of humor, I recommend reading Semiotics. Also, take a look at some of the other reading lists I have posted.

"Nietzsche contra Wagner" by Friedrich Nietzsche
"Art as the Communication of Feeling" from
    What is Art? by Leo Tolstoy
"The Definition of Beauty" from *The Sense of Beauty*
    by George Santayana
The Dehumanization of Art by Jose Ortega y Gasset
"The Work of Art in the Age of Mechanical Reproduction"
    by Walter Benjamin
"Truth and Stereotype" by Ernst Hans Gombrich
"The Origin of the Work of Art" by Martin Heidegger
"Abstract, Representational, and so forth" by
    Clement Greenberg
"Romantic Survival and Revival in the Twentieth Century"
    by Robert Rosemblum

"On the Vernacular of Beauty" by Dave Hickey

"Boring Art" by Frances Colpitt

"The Allegorical Impulse: Toward a Theory of Postmodernism" by Craig Owens

"Modernity: an incomplete project" by Jürgen Habermas

A lecture by George Steiner

Darling of Exhuberance

Friday, November 16, 2007

I am now writing from the Santa Monica studio. We have been working at it for some time and it will be some time still until it is finished.

A rainbow-colored butterfly flies over Dante, Milton, Swedenborg, Blake, Schopenhauer, Nietzsche, Freud, Jung, Heidegger: the flowers of beauty and death. Here is some pollen from Blake.

> You never know what is enough unless you know what is more than enough.

> Exuberance is Beauty.

> The road of excess leads to the palace of wisdom.

> Prudence is a rich ugly old maid courted by Incapacity.

> He who desires but acts not, breeds pestilence.

> The cut worm forgives the plow.

The Prince

Tuesday, November 20, 2007

Richard Prince recently said something along the lines
of "my favorite place is the studio."

It would be nice to see his passion somewhere else
other than the market.

Golden Ratio

Monday, December 3, 2007

I understand the desire for ideal proportions, but the cult of the Golden Ratio seems puzzling to me. For all its divine attributions, the hope for a perfect ratio seems very human, and nowhere are the characteristic limitations, distortions and tenderness of humanity more apparent than in the need to find clues of the definite importance of the Golden Ratio—Fibonacci numbers, pyramids, ideal buildings. In the case of paintings, for instance, it might not make sense to decide shape independently of "content," and once content has been taken into account, other criteria will reveal the secondary importance of an a priori proportion.

Foolishness

Monday, December 3, 2007

The Head of the Extension Program: Don't forget your notes on Beckett. Work hard. Remember: The road of excess leads to the palace of wisdom.

Marty The Fool: It is always a late arrival. And no one is waiting for you at the palace.

The heavy bottom lip of the Head of the Extension Program lost whatever shape it had.

Tall Words

Tuesday, December 4, 2007

I have mentioned earlier on this blog the unnecessary tall words used by galleries on press releases. But the problem is not limited to that type of advertisement. Fancy terminology and confounding statements are, more or less, de rigueur in the art world. The reasons why this is might be illustrative of collective and individual anxieties but rather than explore those, now I just want to suggest we desist on the usage of terminology and postures that are not necessary.

At times, the need for clarity and precision requires terms and methods that might not be familiar to everyone. But arcane notions ought to be tools in the search for truths rather than veils to hide lies. It is more productive to study great thinkers to understand the mechanism of their thought than to find a quotable phrase or a hook for one's deficiencies; even minor understanding of a good mind brings forth humility. The temptation is always there to firm our soft understanding with the prop of the big word or the important framework, but these affectations tend to hide truths not only from others but from ourselves as well.

Partly because philosophy and literature have played a role in my work and are part of my vocabulary, it has been a challenge for me to avoid the failings I have just described. Whatever the excuse, I am disappointed whenever I can't find a way around fancy terminology. I think most people should avoid the embarrassment of sounding like intellectuals—particularly if they are intellectuals.

The End of a Lovely Season

Monday, December 31, 2007

The measurement of time seems more arbitrary than it did before. Seasons come and go, and it is hard to satisfy the hunger of their coming and going.

As my last entry for this year I am including a working excerpt of a conversation between Thomas Hoveling and myself (which in its final version will be included in the catalog for my exhibition in Australia), and a brief description of the weekend workshop I will teach this summer at the Anderson Ranch.

The Lovely Season

[Excerpt from a conversation between Thomas Hoveling and Enrique Martínez Celaya]

"Tell me about the children who appear in many of the recent works," he said while turning on the lamp by his side. I thought about our other conversations about childhood and I wanted to say something new, even if it was not true.

"Everything seems possible with them but also, they might show signs of the many things that will not be possible."

"How about the two sculptures of boys?"

"Maybe they're to the image of a child what a petrified tree is to a tree."

"You don't see these children as symbols?"

"No. I realize there's a tendency to read images as symbols to be decoded though psychological or political machinations, but to me images are flatter. They represent themselves first and foremost. To stop at the thing…," I said fearing I was sliding towards my typical, and dull, philosophical observations.

"Do you think our society is becoming more sophisticated about images as it is often said?" Thomas asked.

"I guess it depends what you mean by sophistication. One way to see our world is as a river of images moving quickly past our consciousness. Everyone is quick with the glimpse and the quick interpretation. But the whole thing is fairly trivial, don't you think?"

"I don't know anything about that world, really. I'm out of the loop," he said.

"The current seems to be moving towards small screens with little movies and a taste more defined by sampling than by sustained engagement; the art fair booth with the one painting by each artist, the music download with the one hit song."

When I finished talking, we remained quietly sitting near each other, while I tried to dissimulate my embarrassment. I shouldn't have been speaking in front of Thomas about the restless spirit of modern life. It must have tested his patience.

"Let's eat," he said.

Stumbling Towards an Artwork that is not as Terrible at it Could Be

[Brief description of the workshop at the Anderson Ranch]

Topics to be discussed include the challenges of making art in the age of careerism and art funds, the struggle between entertainment and art, and the obstacles that help in the formation of an artist. In addition to the lectures, a selection of critiques will be held as a well as a "symposium" between the participants, the artist and his created character, Thomas Hoveling. The "symposium" will include debates with volunteers regarding artistic worldview, question and answer and interviews.

Each day will consist of a lively discussion followed by a critique and/or a directed argument.

Santa Monica Studio

We have finished the construction on the Santa Monica studio, and seeing the effort, some people have asked me if the project takes away from my work.

The question seems to point at a more definite understanding of my work than the one I have. To me, "the work" is always shifting and always feeding on that shift. The question also underestimates the value of this particular "detour." It would be hard for me to make a categorical distinction between the process that generates a painting and the process that decides if I should hang the deer head in the studio's library. In each gesture I am trying to sort myself in relation to it and to find something refuge-like in the final assembly. Space and furniture, for instance, are something quite distinct from the position one takes towards painting only if the purpose itself is quite distinct. For me, the studio is an embodiment of the same point of view that generates the artwork.

The artwork and the studio have many (though not all) of the same aims and provide me with similar comfort and discomfort, so what is the meaning of lost time or interruption of the work? I gain energy by using it.

Soul Searching

Tuesday, February 12, 2008

"A great nation deserves great art" is the slogan of the National Endowment for the Arts. It is catchy but what does it mean?

A nation inches towards greatness, in part, by assuming it doesn't deserve much, and it maintains its greatness, in part, by understanding "greatness" is not a coronation or a title but a reflection of the quality of becoming.

Moreover, the relationship between great art and great nations is by no means tidy. Spain in the Seventeenth Century, for instance, was losing its hold on the empire and was burdened by disease. It was also entrenched in the Inquisition and abusing the American provinces. So did it deserve Velázquez, Zurbarán, Lope de Vega, Luis de Góngora, etc?

Perhaps it is more accurate to say—in the case of Spain as well as in many others—that nations get the soul searching they deserve in the work of their artists. Art is the mirror in which nations who think of themselves as great must see themselves, often, as otherwise. But that is a less catchy slogan.

A Witty Age

Monday, March 17, 2008

The moralists are running to the microphones, their chests inflamed with indignation. They make an example of Eliot Spitzer and their theatrics remind me of that other Eliot, who thought the world would end with a whimper rather than a bang. If only some would avoid speech, as in that other line of "The Hollow Men."

"What an age," Thomas Hoveling once said and then, when I didn't say anything, he added, "Wit. Don't forget the wit."

Here is a little fantasy:

I settle for smelling the orange blossoms as the powdered wigs walk by. Everyone looks so good under the glass tears of the chandeliers. Everyone but me, I say to Thomas, and with a finger smeared in saliva, I remove the dirt from my shoes. I sit in a corner trying to fit in. Experts in irony, the moralists, with their flaring cuffs, hold the little hands of the academics as they glide on the dance floor. The entertainers and the financiers talk about their retirement accounts while the rebels listen in.

I do fit in. And where are the arts?

They wave at me from the other side of the room where a small auction is being held. All of them, even the critics, are wearing Hirst's Manolo Blahniks. On the men, the Manolos seem a bit puffy.

Kierkegaard and The Present Age

Friday, March 21, 2008

An excerpt from Søren Kierkegaard, *The Present Age and of the Difference Between a Genius and an Apostle*, trans. Alexander Dru (New York: Harper Torchbooks, 1962):

> If a precious jewel, which all desired, lay out on a frozen lake, where the ice was perilously thin, where death threatened one who went out too far while the ice near the shore was safe, in a passionate age the crowds would cheer the courage of the man who went out on the ice; they would fear for him and with him in his resolute action; they would sorrow over him if he went under; they would consider him divine if he returned with the jewel. In this passionless, reflective age, things would be different. People would think themselves very intelligent in figuring out the foolishness and worthlessness of going out on the ice, indeed, that it would be incomprehensible and laughable; and thereby they would transform passionate daring into a display of skill…The people would go and watch from safety and the connoisseurs with their discerning tastes would carefully judge the skilled skater, who would go almost to the edge (that is, as far as the ice was safe, and would not go beyond this point) and then swing back. The most skilled skaters would go out the furthest and venture most dangerously, in order to make the crowds gasp and say: "Gods! He is insane, he will kill himself!" But you

will see that his skill is so perfected that he will at the right moment swing around while the ice is still safe and his life is not endangered…

Men, then, only desire money, and money is an abstraction, a form of reflection… Men do not envy the gifts of others, their skill, or the love of their women; they only envy each others' money… These men would die with nothing to repent of, believing that if only they had the money, they might have truly lived and truly achieved something.

The established order continues, but our reflection and passionlessness finds its satisfaction in ambiguity. No person wishes to destroy the power of the king, but if little by little it can be reduced to nothing but a fiction, then everyone would cheer the king. No person wishes to pull down the pre-eminent, but if at the same time pre-eminence could be demonstrated to be a fiction, then everyone would be happy. No person wishes to abandon Christian terminology, but they can secretly change it so that it doesn't require decision or action. And so they are unrepentant, since they have not pulled down anything. People do not desire any more to have a strong king than they do a hero-liberator than they do religious authority, for they innocently wish the established order to continue, but in a reflective way they more or less know that the established order no longer continues…

The reflective tension this creates constitutes itsel into a new principle, and just as in an age of passion enthusiasm is the unifying principle, so in a passionless age of reflection envy is the negative-unifying principle. This must not be understood as a moral term, but rather, the idea of reflection, as it were, is envy, and envy is therefore twofold: it is selfish in the individual and in the society around him. The envy of reflection in the individual hinders any passionate decision he might make; and if he wishes to free himself from reflection, the reflection of society around him re-captures him...

Envy constitutes the principle of characterlessness, which from its misery sneaks up until it arrives at some position, and it protects itself with the concession that it is nothing. The envy of characterlessness never understands that distinction is really a distinction, nor does it understand itself in recognizing distinction negatively, but rather reduces it so that it is no longer distinction; and envy defends itself not only from distinction, but against that distinction which is to come.[7]

The Lucky One

Tuesday, March 25, 2008

Thomas asked me today what had I earned and I answered, "Nothing, everything I got I got by luck."

"That's a fancy, muchacho," he said, "you're not that lucky."

Then I remembered this:

'Till, gaining that vital centre, the black bubble upward burst; and now, liberated by reason of its cunning spring, and, owing to its great buoyancy, rising with great force, the coffin life-buoy shot lengthwise from the sea, fell over, and floated by my side. Buoyed up by that coffin, for almost one whole day and night, I floated on a soft and dirgelike main. The unharming sharks, they glided by as if with padlocks on their mouths; the savage sea-hawks sailed with sheathed beaks. On the second day, a sail drew near, nearer, and picked me up at last. It was the devious-cruising Rachel, that in her retracing search after her missing children, only found another orphan.'[8]

"I guess I earned at least one pleasure," I said.

"That's the one I was thinking about," he said.

The Architect

Tuesday, April 8, 2008

Thomas and I drove to Encinitas to see a juggler who goes by the sobriquet "The Architect." The drive this time of year is pleasant but I was happy when we finally arrived. The show was arranged at an old ranch—the type of production you know had some poet behind it. We sat under a eucalyptus tree with a good view of the stage, which was maybe the size of a small bedroom. The excitement built as the crowd grew, and when The Architect appeared we burst into applause. The Architect was dressed as a nurse, which at first seemed confusing but after a while began to make sense. His entrance was nothing to speak of, and during the show he barely acknowledged the audience. The show, however, was enthralling.

He began with one red ball, which he easily kept in the air, ease he exaggerated by looking at his watch while the ball went up and down. Then he brought in a second ball and about the time that second ball went up, a sudden breeze crossed the stage. The two balls were easy for him but the insistent little wind was definitely disturbing their trajectory. A third ball went up and a fourth. Each new ball exaggerated the unpredictability of the others, but The Architect didn't seem to mind the chaos when four or five or six balls were in the air and his skill was enough to hide the balls' uncertainty. But when the seventh ball went up the situation changed. The Architect's efforts to compensate for the wind became noticeable and his movements lost some of their grace. The ninth ball ended the act.

We were walking towards our car when we saw the juggler coming out from a barn. He was not wearing the nurse uniform but jeans and a t-shirt. Thomas, who likes to talk to everyone, complimented The Architect on the show. The Architect thanked Thomas, said something about the wind, and introduced himself as Rick Gibson.

Being Cuban

Tuesday, May 13, 2008

For some time questions and bewilderment about my "Cubanness" have hovered around my work and me. From what I gather, it seems to some people that my influences, my behavior and public choices, and the way I go about presenting my work do not easily conform to notions of being Cuban, or even Latin American.

Today I will contribute my opinion to this minor debate.

I have often thought that Tolstoy's first line in *Anna Karenina*, "Happy families are all alike; every unhappy family is unhappy in its own way," is not only a fine remark on the specificity of misery but also a warning against the tendency to trust generalizations.

Undoubtedly, ethnicity and nationality contribute to self-definition, but are they as relevant in day-to-day living as our individual experiences of class, family, exile, disease and books, and our happenstance of epoch, encounters and genetics? Furthermore, if we are heirs to values and assumptions that influence the manner in which experiences are lived and perceived, how do the experiences, in turn, influence those values and assumptions? And in the arts, where does heritage begin and end? For instance, in the question of Joseph Conrad's "Russianness," where is Poland, orphanhood, lost nobility, the sea, sickness, exile and language? Is Conrad's Russianness something more than an aroma perfuming the man and his writing? And what in T.S. Eliot is American? Is Pablo Picasso's work Spanish? Is Jorge Luis Borges a traitor for preferring English and German?

I won't attempt to answer any of these questions. Instead I offer them as disclaimers to what follows.

For me, being Cuban is about the tone of my childhood and subsequent exile and, less importantly, some values and fears that colored the way I was raised.

My childhood is a childhood of images I still don't understand and hence, to be Cuban, for me, is to not have been in Cuba long enough to understand them: poorly lit rooms decorated with furniture that couldn't be bought anymore and therefore couldn't be used; standing in dilapidated yards on bright hot days; watching adults mourn our impending departure; talks of "El Norte;" talks of Fidel; surreal juxpositions of old toy soldiers and caged birds and billboards of the revolution; suffocating asthma attacks on a sweaty bed; leaving on an *Iberia* plane knowing we will never go back. To be Cuban is also to have lived in Spain as a foreigner; to have endured the jokes; to have learned to speak with a Castilian accent; to have gone to Mass only to look at the girls; to have been poor in Madrid in winter; to have sought country in my family, compatriots in my brothers and fistfights in school.

To be Cuban is also the Cuban writers who I read as a kid: Guillermo Cabrera Infante, Nicolás Guillén, José Martí, Reinaldo Arenas and Alejo Carpentier; it was the Spanish translations of Kafka and Tolstoy and my mother's choice of reading to me a story about the sinking of the Andrea Doria at nighttime.

I did most of my reading in Puerto Rico, however, where being Cuban meant being an outsider but also a fellow "Caribeño." Caribeño, in the 1970s (and probably still), was being part of the sea, Colonialism, humor, food and a collective sense of inferiority. It was also reading Kant in Junior High School hoping we were smart enough (we weren't) to understand it, but free of the idea that the German philosopher wasn't speaking for us.

To be Cuban, for me, means more sad letters than country, more a way of looking at things and memories. It also means nothing really "is," everything is becoming, including self-definition; every idea can be my own and every failing possible. To be Cuban, for me, is to be thrown into the recognition, as Kristeva has suggested, that the foreigner is within us and that, consequently, what some people don't understand about me and my work—German and Scandinavian influences, American literary references, physics, concerns with time, Jewish parallels—is nothing but an attempt to makes sense of that foreigner.

On Looking at the Work Done

Thursday, June 12, 2008

I find it an impossible book: I consider it badly written, ponderous, embarrassing, image-mad and image-confused, sentimental, in places saccharine to the point of effeminacy, uneven in tempo, without the will to logical cleanliness, very convinced and therefore disdainful of proof, mistrustful even of the propriety of proof, a book for initiates, 'music' for those dedicated to music, those who are closely related to begin with on the basis of common and rare aesthetic experiences, 'music' meant as a sign of recognition for close relatives in arbitus (In the arts)—an arrogant and rhapsodic book that ought to exclude right from the beginning the profanum vulgus (the profane crowd) of 'the educated' even more than 'the mass' or 'folk.'

wrote Nietzsche in regards to his book *The Birth of Tragedy*.[9]

But despite his accusations and reservations Nietzsche found value in his book because he trusted the intent and the merits of its subject (the history of Greek tragedy and the psychological/philosophical distinction between the Dionysian and Apollonian spirits), and also because Nietzsche had an ability (coming from clarity, arrogance or both) to see his own personal enterprise in a historical perspective: "this audacious book dared to tackle for the first time: to look at science in the perspective of the artist, but at art in that of life."[10]

For two years my studio has been working on a series of books documenting the work I have done since my days as an apprentice. It is not a work for publication. Nonetheless, seeing it in the world, even in its limited visibility, makes me consider the value of much of what I have done, and in turn, much of what I am doing. Looking at these books I have feelings not unlike the ones Nietzsche had in regards to *The Birth of Tragedy*, with the exception of his conviction of the work's importance.

There is one argument the books make very convincingly: some things won't be again.

Nietzsche an underpinning to my aesthetic ideal?

Friday, June 13, 2008

In response to gawalt's comment to the previous blog entry.

No. I was trying to distinguish my ambivalence towards the value of work I've done with Nietzsche's certainty.

But your question regarding the underpinnings to my aesthetic ideal is interesting.

It might be Nietzschean but it is difficult to say, particularly because Nietzsche's aesthetics and his views about the function of art changed throughout his life.

When I was younger I read Nietzsche and other authors influenced by his ideas. Those readings had an impact on me, among other things because they came at the right time and because I didn't have a well-developed frame of reference. So I think it is likely that to some extent Nietzsche has influenced my work—possibly to a large extent—but the way in which his ideas influenced my work and thought are indistinguishable now from the foundation of my point of view. I probably read him too early.

It makes me think of an old friend who, regarding the books of Hermann Hesse, said: *Demian* is a book that should only be read when you are starting your life and *Steppenwolf* a book that should only be read when you are coming back from life. I am not sure what he meant but it sounds right.

As a youth it is easier to feel comfortable with adoring Nietzsche.

The Hand

Wednesday, July 16, 2008

When I cut my left hand the words from the Hagakure, "At that time is right now," came to mind. As I looked at the hand, life was both—and not contradictorily—more factual and more dreamlike, and what was happening was no longer in the future but right there. The first part, the taking off the glove, was the hardest. Once I had seen it, there was nothing but coming to terms with things.

It happened while I was carving a large wood sculpture. I was going back and forth between a chainsaw and a high-speed grinder equipped with a chainsaw blade, which allowed me to move quickly through the wood. I almost remember the moment when my hand touched the blade but I remember better the moment just before and just after.

My life will soon continue, more or less, as it was. The turn, however, did happen; in my case a minor turn, for which I am grateful. The turn has been worse for others. In the ambulance I couldn't stop thinking about the people losing body parts in Iraq—the American soldiers, the Iraqis, the children. The images that came to my mind seemed then—as they do now—unjustifiable by any policy or by any excuse.

Right now, someone, somewhere, holds on to his or her dismembered leg, arm or hand, or to the dismembered part of a daughter, a father, or a friend. That we can know that and continue on with our banal lives clearly says something about the machinery of survival.

Nature's Silence

Friday, July 18, 2008

This entry is in response to Cory's comment and to similar questions I have been asked in the past.

Cory wrote: "To me, what is important in art is reaching deep into the silence of nature's 'building.' I do not find theoretical understanding of art helpful in this pursuit, and I really just want to know if you do."

I think I understand the spirit of the question but I disagree with its underlying premise. The question, consciously or unconsciously, frames an opposition between "the silence" and reason, an opposition that, in most cases, comes from prejudices about the nature and use of reason as well as "the silence." I don't think we are able to reach into "the silence of nature's building" but it might be possible to sense aspects of what I think Cory means by "the silence."

However, I haven't met too many people who have a direct channel to this silence, or perhaps it is more accurate to say I haven't met many people whose claim to direct channels seem credible. Any help in clarifying one's work—theoretical or not—is good and necessary because, for the most part, we are lost. Each of us has ways and methods we prefer—as it should be. Of course, there is a time for everything; a time for theory and a time for doing; a time for looking and a time for not looking.

The Hand (II)

Monday, September 8, 2008

I should come back to the blog by getting the hand out of the way.

My hand is doing well. So well in fact, it is hard to lay the memory of what it looked like on what it looks like now. More importantly, my hand is fully functional.

The credit for this small miracle goes to Dr. Jerry Yoram Haviv, a surgeon who practices in Santa Monica, California. When I arrived at the hospital following the accident, the surgeon in charge said, "If this had happened to me, I would want Dr. Haviv to be my surgeon."

Dr. Haviv's seriousness and palpable intelligence impressed me right away. I was also pleased to see he carried his magnifying glasses in a small, old-world, wooden box. He introduced himself, removed the bandages wrapped around my hand, studied the bloody fingers and told me what he was planning to do. What Dr. Haviv said was more promising than I expected and what he did was even better. In the last few months, I have looked forward to his evaluations of my progress and to our talks about art, Israel and books.

The Scholar

Tuesday, September 9, 2008

The following quotes are from E.M. Forster's *Aspects of the Novel*.

The scholar, like the philosopher, can contemplate the river of time. He contemplates it not as a whole, but he can see the facts, the personalities, floating past him, and estimate the relations between them, and if his conclusions could be as valuable to us as they are to himself he would long ago have civilized the human race. As you know, he has failed. True scholarship is incommunicable, true scholars rare. There are a few scholars, actual or potential, in the audience today, but only a few, and there is certainly none on the platform. Most of us are pseudo-scholars, and I want to consider our characteristics with sympathy and respect, for we are a very large and quite a powerful class, eminent in Church and State, we control the education of the Empire, we lend to the Press such distinction as it consents to receive, and we are a welcome asset at dinner-parties.

Pseudo-scholarship is, on its good side, the homage paid by ignorance to learning.

Everything he says may be accurate but all is useless, because he is moving round books instead of through them, he either has not read them or cannot read them properly. Books have to be read (worse luck, for it takes a long time); it is the only way of discovering what they may contain. [...] The reader must sit down alone and struggle with the writer, and this the pseudo-scholar will not do. He would rather relate a book to the history of its time, to events in the life of its author, to the events it describes, above all to some tendency. As soon as he can use the word "tendency" his spirits rise, and though those of his audience may sink, they often pull out their pencils at this point and make a note, under the belief that a tendency is portable.[11]

Spin Paintings

Tuesday, September 16, 2008

In contrast to the perspective offered by distance, our daily living favors the immediate and the fashionable, and sometimes persuaded by that immediacy as well as by cultural repetition and the desire to seem informed, people praise the artistic merit of dubious artworks, and moral flexibility and status anxiety encourage these colorful evaluations.

On September 15, 2008, the same day the Stock Market lost more than 500 points, partly as a result of whimsical investments in the financial field gone bad, more than 200 pieces of new work by Damien Hirst sold through Sotheby's for more than 200 million dollars. The offering of pickled animals, butterflies and dots, which were made by the more than 180 people who work for Hirst, was the first time an artist used an auction house to sell new work. Hirst's action and it's success are part of a larger condition, which Robert Hughes appropriately described in the following way:

> Where you see Hirsts you will also see Jeff Koons's balloons, Jean-Michel Basquiat's stoned scribbles, Richard Prince's feeble jokes and pin-ups of nurses and, inevitably, scads of really bad, really late Warhols. Such works of art are bound to hang out together, a uniform message from our fin-de-siècle decadence.[12]

Some of us feel like hypocrites when we call for ambition of spirit and authenticity in the work of art, knowing we don't ask for the same in our own lives. And so we learn to accept trivial and cowardly gestures as significant and brave because in them we sense our own failings. We become practiced in self-serving praise of the meager and the vicious, but irrespectively of these moral accommodations, when time has passed and our fears and status no longer matter, the diamond-encrusted skulls and spin paintings will become, mainly, symbols of our dishonesty and lack of clarity.

What we need in art is ambition of spirit, quality and authenticity, not because those imperatives are abundant in our lives but precisely because they are not.

The Freedom to Be

Thursday, September 18, 2008

In the essay "The Wisdom of Life" Schopenhauer writes,

Everyone believes himself a priori to be perfectly free, even in his individual actions, and thinks that at every moment he can commence another manner of life... But a posteriori, through experience, he finds to his astonishment that he is not free, but subjected to necessity, that in spite of all his resolutions and reflections he does not change his conduct, and that from the beginning of his life to the end of it, he must carry out the very character which he himself condemns...[13]

On T.S. Eliot's Birthday

Friday, September 26, 2008

Let's celebrate T.S. Eliot's birthday. Here is Section I of
"Ash Wednesday." The entire poem is available online.

Because I do not hope to turn again
Because I do not hope
Because I do not hope to turn
Desiring this man's gift and that man's scope
I no longer strive to strive towards such things
(Why should the aged eagle stretch its wings?)
Why should I mourn
The vanished power of the usual reign?

Because I do not hope to know
The infirm glory of the positive hour
Because I do not think
Because I know I shall not know
The one veritable transitory power
Because I cannot drink
There, where trees flower, and springs flow, for there is
    nothing again

Because I know that time is always time
And place is always and only place
And what is actual is actual only for one time
And only for one place
I rejoice that things are as they are and
I renounce the blessed face

And renounce the voice
Because I cannot hope to turn again
Consequently I rejoice, having to construct something
Upon which to rejoice

And pray to God to have mercy upon us
And pray that I may forget
These matters that with myself I too much discuss
Too much explain
Because I do not hope to turn again
Let these words answer
For what is done, not to be done again
May the judgement not be too heavy upon us

Because these wings are no longer wings to fly
But merely vans to beat the air
The air which is now thoroughly small and dry
Smaller and dryer than the will
Teach us to care and not to care Teach us to sit still.

Pray for us sinners now and at the hour of our death
Pray for us now and at the hour of our death.

Unreasonable Pursuits: Moby-Dick

Tuesday, October 14, 2008

The reasonableness of most pursuits is arguable, especially pursuits carried consciously or unconsciously as affronts to reasonableness. In the arts, but not just in the arts, these reasonableness-challenging pursuits tend to lead far from certainty. The mighty and the ones who like to appear mighty or who don't know any better, suggest trusting, advice that has kept many in foolish voyages from which they never returned. The prudent and the cowards suggest retreating and the results of this advice are plain to see.

It is not easy to be a good judge of time and circumstance, which is what is called for here. The following are excerpts from contemporary reviews of *Moby-Dick* and from a note on Melville's death (from www.melville.org, a useful website). I find it interesting to read these from a distance of 150 years, which we don't have in our own pursuits.

"The more careful, therefore, should he [Herman Melville] be to maintain the fame he so rapidly acquired, and not waste his strength on such purposeless and unequal doings as these rambling volumes about spermaceti whales."

—*London Literary Gazette*, December 6, 1851

"In all other aspects, the book is sad stuff, dull and dreary, or ridiculous. Mr. Melville's Quakers are the wretchedest dolts and drivellers, and his Mad Captain ...is a monstrous bore."
—*Charleston Southern Quarterly Review*, January 1852

"We have no intention of quoting any passages just now from Moby Dick...But if there are any of our readers who wish to find examples of bad rhetoric, involved syntax, stilted sentiment and incoherent English, we will take the liberty of recommending to them this precious volume of Mr. Melville's."
 —*New York United States Magazine and Democratic Review*, January 1852

"It is strange how he persists—and has persisted ever since I knew him, and probably long before—in wondering to-and-fro over these deserts, as dismal and monotonous as the sand hills amid which we were sitting. He can neither believe, nor be comfortable in his unbelief; and he is too honest and courageous not to try to do one or the other. If he were a religious man, he would be one of the most truly religious and reverential; he has a very high and noble nature, and better worth immortality than most of us."
—Nathaniel Hawthorne, *Notebook Entry*, November 20, 1856

"The sum and substance of our fault-finding with Herman Melville is this. He has indulged himself in a trick of metaphysical and morbid meditations until he has almost perverted his fine mind from its healthy productive tendencies."

—Fitz-James O'Brien: "Our Authors and Authorship, Melville and Curtis." In *Putnam's Monthly Magazine* (New York), April 1857

"Herman Melville, one of the most original and virile of American literary men, died at his home on Twenty-sixth street, New York, a few days ago, at the age of 72. He had long been forgotten, and was no doubt unknown to the most of those who are reading the magazine literature and the novels of the day. Nevertheless, it is probable that no work of imagination more powerful and often poetic has been written by an American than Melville's romance of Moby Dick; or the Whale, published just 40 years ago [...] Certainly it is hard to find a more wonderful book than this Moby Dick, and it ought to be read by this generation, amid whose feeble mental food, furnished by the small realists and fantasts of the day, it would appear as Hercules among the pygmies, or as Moby Dick himself among a school of minnows."

—Springfield, *Massachusetts Republican*, October 4, 1891

A Sentimental Education

Tuesday, October 21, 2008

Sometimes I am asked about my influences or my education, and I sometimes ask others for the same. I am not sure what we expect to find. Causes and effects are usually separated by years and events; a bent here; a twist there; a fear, for instance, that reacts with an image or a song to make a new emotional compound and part of a personality. The stories we build to make sense of what happens or happened are fictions, always oversimplified and often misunderstood.

In 1978, Pablo and I had a sleepover and as part of the rituals we ate late, talked—mostly lied—about girls, and played records. I think Pablo had gotten the records from his father. Through the night Paco Ibañez, Silvio Rodriguez and Joan Manuel Serrat sang and we listened pretending to be more mature than we were; at fourteen we could still take ourselves seriously. At some point we played Serrat's record devoted to the poems of Miguel Hernandez and lay on the floor looking up at the ceiling, in silence. Since then "Umbrío por la Pena" has been an ongoing education.

Umbrío por la Pena

Umbrío por la pena, casi bruno,
porque la pena tizna cuando estalla,
donde yo no me hallo no se halla
hombre más apenado que ninguno.

Sobre la pena duermo solo y uno,
pena es mi paz y pena mi batalla,
perro que ni me deja ni se calla,
siempre a su dueño fiel, pero importuno.

Cardos y penas llevo por corona,
cardos y penas siembran sus leopardos
y no me dejan bueno hueso alguno.

No podrá con la pena mi persona
rodeada de penas y de cardos:
¡cuánto penar para morirse uno!

Shadowed by Sorrow

Shadowed by sorrow, nearly black
because sorrow soots when it bursts,
where I am not, it is not
the most sorrowed man.

I sleep alone and one on the sorrow,
sorrow is my peace and sorrow my battle;
a dog that neither leaves nor lies quiet,
always faithful, but inopportune.

Thistles and pain I carry as a crown,
thistles and pain sow leopards
that do not leave a bone uncrushed.

Surrounded by sorrow and thistles
my body can bear no more.
So much sorrow only to die!

[In translating this poem I used Ted Genoway's
translation as a starting point.]

Mayakovsky, Mandelstam and Barnes

Friday, October 31, 2008

Two interesting poetry events.

1. Whale & Star's recent publication of *Mandelstam: Modernist Archaist*.[14] The book's editor, Kevin M. F. Platt, assembled new translations by notable contemporary poets combined with an exceptional selection of previous translations.

2. Thomas tells me that one night in the winter of 1978 Clifford Barnes was holding fort at the White Horse Tavern, where from time to time Cliff lowered his voice, looked at one of his admirers in the eyes and delivered a bit of wisdom. He wielded his softness like a flamethrower and that annoyed Vladimir Mayakovsky, who was drinking quietly nearby. Mayakovsky told Cliff to shut up but the bard, not used to people like the Georgian, smirked, which cost him a beating.

Painting and Structure

Why does an image work in a painting while another (a similar one, say) does not? What is the balance between presence and reference and on what does that balance depend? How is distance created in the interaction between viewer and painting and is it possible to speak of the autonomy of a painting?

Usually, painting is seen mostly for the amalgam of attributes that it is, such as treatment, imagery, scale, etc—painting as a sum of sorts. However, if instead of seeing painting as sum we look at it singularly as a state of thought, our view of painting and how it is achieved can change in significant ways. Most of the issues that matter, for instance, will quickly show themselves to be related to structure. That is, related to the underlying supports that give shape to the state of thought, and by thought here I mean the entire force of the spirit: reason, emotion, intuition, etc.

I will try to write more about this in the future.

Radical Doubting

People vary in their capacity for accepting doubt, especially of cherished beliefs, and they also vary in how much of themselves they are willing to doubt.

The belief that our experience, our education, our status and our upbringing are proofs and guarantees is vanity. Although never easy, it seems clear that erasing some aspect of attributes-of-self is necessary. *In Fear and Trembling,* Kierkegaard quotes Luke 14:26: "If anyone comes to me and does not hate his father and mother, his wife and children, his brothers and sisters— yes, even his own life—he cannot be my disciple."[15]

What does one trust? I have considered this question for a long time but neither the question nor its implications have become easier. Some time ago I read Alan Watts: "To have faith is to trust yourself to the water. When you swim you don't grab hold of the water, because if you do you will sink and drown. Instead you relax, and float."[16]

Relax and float.

Yet, while relaxing and floating are necessary, they are not sufficient; at least not for doing something interesting and meaningful—admittedly values. To do, and perhaps also to be, something interesting and meaningful, passion and faith must exist as well. Art, like life, depends in part on desperate passion and faith amid unshakable doubts. A leap of faith must not only be taken despite doubts but in fact depends on those doubts. There is no leap without doubts.

While faith—the confidence of a better condition—is probably always spiritual in essence, ought not to be religious in practice, in discipline. Of course, without religious doctrine, as if the case in art, passion and faith often become soft and end up being more attributes of vanity. In my view, the crucial word in the previous paragraph is "desperate."

Radical doubting.

Structure (I)

Wednesday, December 17, 2008

Some artists consider structure the most exciting aspect of art and while others might not go that far, it is hard to imagine a musician, artist or writer who is not frequently puzzled by an aspect of structure. To consider structure in the visual arts, literature, dance, and music means to take on the relationship between parts and whole, between forces and constraints, between the "in" and "out" of the work. That is, to consider structure is to consider why something works or doesn't, and since art is only that which works, to consider its working is to consider its essence.

This might be why many visual artists have tried to make structure more explicit in their artwork and why frankness about structure has become expected in most intellectual circles. In fact, structure is one of the foci around which the 250 year-old Modern project revolves. In the last century, the desire to make structure more explicit led a significant number of artists to take structure—somewhat isolated from other aspects of art—as the subject of their work. The effort of the isolationists has, at times, produced work of subtlety and insight and, other times, the work has been mired by cleverness. In either case, the results—for the most part—only have the appearance of art.

Structure (II)

Tuesday, December 23, 2008

It is probably the crudest but also the truest approximation to say what matters in art is Heart. If we were Tilman Riemenschneider, Heart will bring forth and organize, heighten and shape, as it should be. If we are not Tilman Riemenschneider, Heart might not be the fountain or the guide we wish it to be and, for the most part, little can be done about that.

Which might be why anything I say about art or its making often sounds like nonsense to me. In the *Philosophical Investigations*, Wittgenstein wrote:

> We have got onto slippery ice where there is no friction and so in a certain sense the conditions are ideal, but also, just because of that, we are unable to walk. We want to walk so we need friction. Back to the rough ground![17]

The pull towards objective understanding is the fool's effort. The Heart, however, is slippery ice. No work can be done there. The nonsense is the rough ground. Most of my own efforts to understand are centered on concerns with structure, and the main problem I have with the isolationists I mentioned in the previous entry is their structures are seldom complex enough.

A particular structure is a state of the work of art, a state that can be changed by content, purpose and failure. The tensions and points of support in the painting "of an apple" have to be different than those "of a horizon" and then they have to be different if it is "this apple" or "that apple," handled "like this" or "like that" and so on. For instance, an apple painted by Cezanne exerts less "outward" pressure on the surface than one by Van Heem, and therefore brings about an entirely different armature or structure; a green apple is different than a red one; a mythic one is different than a "factual" one. Which is why there is little chance of doing anything useful with general ideas about structure or simplifying its "physics" to perceptual illusions and formal aspects, particularly aspects imagined to be invariant to content, purpose and failure. Structure is the ensemble of forces and parts in the work of art and these forces and parts are re-made by perturbations of everything that matters to the work and its experience.

Perturbations are the type of elusive thing Heart can account for. There is also some sort of "dark matter," invisible to most of us, in the ensemble of forces and parts. Heart finds itself in this uncertainty and this finding re-organizes both.

Heart

Friday, December 26, 2008

Since I barely have ten hours of experience with the boat, Thomas sailed us through the rough Boynton Beach Inlet. As the sea widened, I noticed the whitecaps and looked at Thomas, who was smiling. Talking was hard to do so I sank in the bow seat and enjoyed the fire of the late-afternoon sky. Against the ocean and everything that comes with it, including the birds, many of my writings on this blog seemed flimsy. But not the bit about Heart, though it might be confusing and likely to be misunderstood. What Heart might be was clear as I watched Thomas head into the waves. It was clear in a way my writing wasn't, and it was a clarity no intellectual machinery could diffuse. I blamed my writing and moved on to the walls of dark water rising above us. The wind had picked up and soon Thomas and I were both soaked. The night was almost upon us. I thought of asking him to turn around but the warm water felt good. We were in the Gulf Stream. Maybe if I were Hemingway or Dewey I could write about Heart, I thought. Really? My shortcomings aside, not even Kierkegaard, who did as good of a job as anyone, could make much sense of Heart in words. Pointing towards a cloud. Hand waiving. That's all we have. And examples. Thomas, for me.

Structure (III)

Friday, January 9, 2009

"I am interested then only in the problem of painting, of how to make a better painting according to certain laws that are inherent in the making of a good picture and not at all in private extraversions or introversions of specific individuals,"[18] wrote Marsden Hartley in his 1928 essay "Art and the Personal Life," and for the rest of his career he would claim disdain for the personal, the confessional and the emotional.

But anyone who considers a Marsden Hartley painting with some attention recognizes the man, not just the intellect—personally, emotionally and as a confession. What Hartley might be doing is playing a hide-and-seek game most artists play. Thomas once told me the key to an artist's work is in what he or she denies. It is also possible, though unlikely, that Hartley could have underestimated how much the irrational and rational depend on each other. Whatever the case was, his words exaggerate the opposition of emotion and intellect and of content and form. In contrast, Hartley's paintings make a great argument for—and are—a reconciliation of imagination and the world, of form and content and of the rational and irrational. The structure of his work owes its intelligence not only to a great intellect but to a profound emotional sensitivity that can be perceived throughout.

He concluded his essay in an appropriately confusing and reconciliatory manner:

> Underlying all sensible works of art, there must be somewhere in evidence the particular problems understood. It was so with those artists of the great past who had the intellectual knowledge of structure upon which to place their emotions. It is this structural beauty that makes the old painting valuable. And so it becomes to me a problem. I would rather be sure that I had placed two colors in true relationship to each other than to have exposed a wealth of emotionalism gone wrong in the name of richness of personal expression. For this reason I believe that it is more significant to keep one's painting in a condition of severe experimentalism than to become a quick success by means of cheap repetition.
>
> The real artists have always been interested in this problem, and you feel it strongly in the work of Da Vinci, Piero della Francesca, Courbet, Pissarro, Seurat, and Cezanne. Art is not a matter of slavery to the emotion or even a matter of slavery to nature or to the aesthetic principles. It is a tempered and happy union of them all.[19]

The Great Commission

Wednesday, January 14, 2009

In 1904 Hilma was informed, through Ananda, that she was to execute paintings on the astral plane. This involved paintings that represented the imperishable. In the summer 1905 she was promised that she would be prepared to mediate a message. The names Amaliel, Ester and Georg were mentioned. It was said that she was to work in service of the mysteries carrying out the new building also called the Temple. First she had to go through a cleansing process. Amaliel said: You shall be struck blind. You shall deny yourself so that your pride shall be broken. You shall stumble in order to be tested for your own weakness. A crying voice shall you become, but before that you shall be broken down into dust.[20]

[Excerpt from the The Hilma af Klint Foundation website]

Failure

Friday, January 23, 2009

In the depressed Puerto Rico of the late 70s, no event was as anticipated as the visit of tightrope walker Karl Wallenda; except perhaps Lou Ferrigno's promised appearance at Safari Park. But since Ferrigno never showed up (the Hulk had to be impersonated by El Tigre Pérez), Wallenda's visit remains the key event of the end of that dreamy decade.

Karl Wallenda, then 73 years old, tried to walk, without a safety net, on a tightrope stretched between two towers in Condado, a hotel area near San Juan. My brothers and I watched him on live TV as he began his act and we kept on watching when he tried to get a grip on the tightrope and when he fell. Every part of that walk and his attempt at a grip had a different quality than anything we had seen before. For us, kids at the time, Wallenda's struggle meant more because he had no safety net.

In recent years, it has become fashionable among certain circles, particularly of academic, crafty and self-help-inclined artists, to speak of failure as a welcomed part of the studio practice. What is often meant by failure here is the loose mental amalgam of it's-ok-if-it-doesn't-work philosophy, some fetishistic concern with process and an excuse for not doing better. Although it is camouflaged as freedom, failure, in this view, is more often than not a form of preciousness, a walk on the tightrope when the risk is small. Failures when the rope is only a few feet from the ground or when there is a safety net are but refreshing winds. These winds, of course, become something else when the rope is raised.

More on Failure

Let me expand on the previous entry.

What is failure without desperateness?

From the *Hagakure* (best read if under a portrait of Søren Kierkegaard):

> Lord Naoshige said, "The Way of the Samurai is in desperateness. Ten men or more cannot kill such a man. Common sense will not accomplish great things. Simply become insane and desperate.
>
> In the Way of the Samurai, if one uses discrimination, he will fall behind. One needs neither loyalty nor devotion, but simply to become desperate in the Way. Loyalty and devotion are of themselves within desperation."
>
> In the judgment of the elders, a samurai's obstinacy should be excessive. A thing done with moderation may later be judged to be insufficient. I have heard that when one thinks he has gone too far, he will not have erred. This sort of rule should not be forgotten.[21]

And one more, also from the *Hagakure*:

> When someone is giving you his opinion, you should receive it with deep gratitude even though it is worthless.[22]

Meltingly sweet, in autumn

Tuesday, February 3, 2009

The meek and fluffy and beautiful world of ours, this world of contrasts, has best been summarized in a recent article about birds in *The Economist*: "Four decades after the campaign, sparrows remained scarcer in Beijing than they should have been (though they could reliably be found being grilled on bamboo skewers in the night markets, along with yellow-breasted buntings, meltingly sweet, in autumn)."[23]

I think in the last few entries I have been circumnavigating my discomfort with the whininess, arrogance and fraud that has so pervasively invaded our lives. Many of us have a ready justification for why we are less than we could be and a way to look at things that makes us think we are really more than what we have become.

The effort of much of growing up seems to be the search for a little tool we can use not to carve our way out of our hole but to dig ourselves deeper. In this narrowing effort we are open minded in the help we recruit, which we find in religion; in the way we were raised; in our power in the world; in our powerlessness; in the pity we feel for ourselves; in the pride we feel for what we have done; in the busyness of our affairs and our job and our lives. We find it in the angelic conversion offered by tattooed wings. Maybe we especially find it there.

But all that is foolish talk. That master or charlatan of extreme wakefulness, G. Gurdjieff, wrote, "Everything is dependent on everything else, everything is connected, nothing is separate. Therefore everything is going in the only way it can go. If people were different everything would be different. They are what they are, so everything is as it is."[24]

So we are left with this (and it could be worse): "They could reliably be found being grilled on bamboo skewers in the night markets, along with yellow-breasted buntings, meltingly sweet, in autumn."

Innocent Fraud

Thursday, February 5, 2009

Paul Krugman, last year's Nobel Prize winner in economics, has been critical of the late, noted economist John Kenneth Galbraith because, among other things, Galbraith wrote for the public rather than for other economists and because Galbraith's economic insights were, at times, over-simplified. These criticisms seem curious to me. Paul Krugman is not only a Princeton professor, but also a columnist for the *New York Times*, a public venue, and a blogger, also a public venue. In addition, Krugman is a frequent contributor to CNN and MSNBC, where the public sound byte is necessarily more over-simplified than anything Galbraith ever wrote. While I agree with much of what Krugman has to say about economics and policy, I detect something akin to ethical envy in his suspicious criticism of Galbraith. Paul Krugman appears to be a man of integrity (his brief role as advisor to Enron can be discounted), however, I think—and Krugman might feel—that it is hard for most of us to measure up to John Kenneth Galbraith. Few can deny that catering to the public is often done at the expense of quality. Yet, Galbraith was not a caterer. In relation to the public, he was an educator and a conscience whose ethics were maintained at a cost to himself and his reputation.

The criticism of writing for the public rather than for the professionals is not merely snobbery, but there is a lot of snobbery in it, which is often misguided and shortsighted. I am reminded of the criticism Wittgenstein—in whom I am interested—launched on Bertrand Russell for wasting his talent by writing books like *The Conquest of Happiness*. While it might be true *The Conquest of Happiness* is not exactly *Principia Mathematica*, it is a gift to be able to observe a good mind like Russell's tackle something mundane but relevant to our lives. We have a long way to go until all we need to think about is the foundation of mathematics or the economics of trade, and if the thinking of the everyday is left only to Dr. Phil, Joel Osteen and Britney Spears, we are in trouble.

Moreover, the world would have benefited from some "public" writing by Wittgenstein, particularly on his moral struggles, which never saw print, academic or otherwise. The problem of talking about something vs. showing it notwithstanding, the opportunity to see the mind of *The Philosophical Investigations*[25] deal with the cumbersome challenges of living and making choices would have been wonderful.

Snobbery is an aspect of any community of experts— including the arts—and it must be understood as the result of educated judgment, convention and self-validation. It would be difficult to argue that the popular appeal of Peter Max or Thomas Kinkade is some sort of confirmation of their greatness. But it is also difficult to argue—although many have tried—that the unpopularity of something or its popularity are diagnostic of its quality. Take, for instance, the complicated case of Andrew Wyeth. The late pictures, particularly the Helga series, are not great but he was undoubtedly a better—and arguably more innovative— painter than most of the celebrated titans of the last fifty years. But it is hard for the art world experts to get excited about an artist whose images have been made into posters for college dorms.

A Gray Stain

Tuesday, February 10, 2009

Then a gray stain appeared on the horizon. It blurred the edge between sky and land until there was only darkness.

Since he had started the new paintings the appeal of something new had grown within him. It was not newness he was after—though at times he inspected its benefits—but the shudder he felt when the dark locomotive of things burst through the barricade of The Known. Yet that morning, after the drunkenness of promise had worn off, the sobriety of familiarity weighed on him. Familiarity, rather than being a mark of authenticity had become a measure of his lack of originality and with this realization his earlier elation gave way to despair. He lay on the painted floor and looked up to the tall shelves and the fluorescent lights. He needed to let someone in.

The Clever Fountain

Monday, March 2, 2009

A meditation on art, influence, expertise, intelligence and opportunism:

Marcel Duchamp's *Fountain* was—and remains—ambiguous. Is it a re-framing of art away from the object and towards concept and interpretation? Or is it an example of art's capacity to incorporate everything into itself? Or is it a joke? In 1964, forty-seven years after being created and lost, the ambiguity of *Fountain* and its maker went up a notch when Arturo Schwarz, Duchamp's European dealer at the time, sold the urinal as an edition. Duchamp, who signed the urinal multiples, felt they represented an inversion of his process: each readymade—like traditional sculpture—individually hand-crafted.

One of these editioned urinals sold at auction in 2002 for $1,762,500, and in 2004, *Fountain* was named the most influential modern artwork of all time by a survey of 500 experts.

Art & the University

Wednesday, April 22, 2009

I have not written for this blog in some time because I have been absorbed by the world of a new cycle of paintings and writings. Today's entry is an excerpt from my recent lecture at the University of Nebraska titled "Art & the University." If you are interested, the complete text of this lecture as well as the other lectures I have prepared during my three-year appointment will be published by the University of Nebraska Press in the fall of 2010.

Excerpt from "Art & the University:"

The scenario I have briefly outlined is symptomatic of our age, an age in which art has more kinship with entertainment and leisure than with religion and science. The age sets the tone but most of us are unaware of the way in which it affects our actions and our dreams. We artists believe in our free will as we hurry to become jesters in the minor court of the artworld.

Looking around faculty or student exhibitions, or, say, at the Saatchi collection in London, we see variety and we convince ourselves it is proof will and whimsy matter more than the age. But we see variety because we are so thoroughly imbedded in our age it has become indistinguishable from ourselves. One hundred years from now, those personal and media variations will be less visible, and two hundred years after that most artworks will lay dormant under the blanket of their age. If it is partly true that as Max Weber wrote, a work of art "is never rendered obsolete by a subsequent work of art," as it is the case in science, it is also true that most works of art rarely transcend the time and the place in which they were made. Weber's work, for instance, seems well anchored in its time.[26]

An Incomplete Reading List on Death

Monday, April 27, 2009

I am posting an incomplete list of novels and two sets of poems touching on death.

Seven novels,

La familia de Pascual Duarte by Camilo José Cela
The Death of Ivan Ilyich by Leo Tolstoy
Anna Karerina by Leo Tolstoy
Moby Dick by Herman Melville
El túnel by Ernesto Sabato
The Death of a Nobody by Jules Romains
The Year of the Death of Ricardo Reis by José Saramago

And two sets of poems,

Platero y yo by Juan Ramón Jiménez
    (a good reason to learn Spanish)
The Yellow Heart by Pablo Neruda

You and the Kindle

Tuesday, April 28, 2009

It is not surprising that factors influencing status anxiety dominated the goofy article about the Kindle written by someone named Joanne Kaufman in the *New York Times* on April 24. The article revolved around different versions of the following paragraph:

> The practice of judging people by the covers of their books is old and time-honored. And the Kindle, which looks kind of like a giant white calculator, is the technology equivalent of a plain brown wrapper. If people jettison their book collections or stop buying new volumes, it will grow increasingly hard to form snap opinions about them by wandering casually into their living rooms.[27]

Yet there are other issues beyond Kaufman's article—beyond status anxiety—to consider regarding the Kindle. The most important is whether or not the Kindle will succeed, because of what its success will mean to publishing and to reading.

It seems certain that—even with that name—the Kindle or another Kindle-like reader will succeed. There are at least four reasons why the Kindle will be unstoppable: 1. It celebrates you (user customization); 2. It celebrates money (new products, new markets);

3. It celebrates democracy (softens the barriers of publishing); 4. It celebrates convenience. For these and other reasons, all but the most obscure books will soon be available for the Kindle.

For some, this triumph will be a confirmation of the righteousness of the electronic reader—the future is written by the winners. But to me the certainty of this success, like the success of many other things of doubtful merit, is only a prediction of the way things go. I love books. I like to understand the moment and the context in which they were printed—a war, a failed state, a surge of revolutionary fervor. I like to see that moment and that context in the paper, in the typeface. My library is not something to show someone else but a useful mirror. When I look at my books, I see my history, choices and accidents. I see the worn edges of books I kept in my pockets in high school. I see my teachers. I see random events that brought a book to me or I see a book I shared with someone else. I see special editions of a novel I sought out because of its etchings, I open my books to find notes in the cover sheets, paint and ink stains on the pages, loose pieces of paper with drawings, or hotel receipts. I see effort. I also like that books are someone else's vision. Not just the vision of the writer but the vision of the publisher, the designer, the printer, the age, the tyrants who tried to stop them, the old bookstore that tried to sell them, and so on. Books are content in context.

The Kindle is about content. Content that is convenient and customizable. Freedom to customize and interact (undoubtedly, a form of electronic context will be available at some point) is at the center of the Internet creed, which is part of what makes the Kindle appealing. The Kindle also facilitates content distribution by eliminating the cost and restrictions of publishing, and it is likely most books will soon be published without a gatekeeper (such as I am doing now)—directly from author to Kindle. You will determine what gets published and you will be able to modify the content *you* like to *your* liking.

Those attributes of the Kindle are supposed to be good things.

The invisible hand of those who make money from *you being you* notwithstanding, I find the contemporary importance of YOU, silly, manipulative and encouraging of mediocrity. Much of what's underneath this self-preoccupation is the infantile desire to be pleased—all the time—as well as the notion that our opinions and desires have particular importance, even if we know very little. Knowledge is increasingly becoming something that comes from the gut and/or opinions.

Perhaps not surprisingly, the YOU that made the cover of *Time* magazine a few years back and that is in the mouth of so many, is nothing too deep. For the most part it is a shell of cravings, prejudices and hang ups that—as many who had tried know—resist dismantling.

This *you* is a farce but trying to dismantle it is painful and, almost always, futile.

Which it might be why we are moving in the other direction. In our age we are stressing the importance of *you*. You know better. You choose. You define. You tell. You decide. Perhaps, as some contemporary thinkers argue, this concentration on *you* is the only way to transcend *you*. They are hoping for a Big Bang. One outcome of this emphasis on *you* is the suspicion of external expertise. Warhol might have missed the point: we all want—and now can have—our fifteen minutes of expertise. Everyone has a say. Everyone is an expert.

As it relates to books, this democratization and celebration of *you* will generate a few nuggets of value—mostly those now in regular books—lost in a thick soup of insignificant knowledge and waste. The search engines will then let you find the parts of the soup that appeal not to some snobbish New York publisher but to *you*. *You* will suck these soup-parts into *your* Kindle and maybe write a blog for the world to know what parts are most important to *you*. Maybe *you* will hope the parts *you* found will be important also to *your* readers—to those who follow *you*. *You* might argue this is not the force-feeding of authority but the sharing of peers; not the tyranny of the oppressor but the democratization of knowledge. *You* have something to say.

You also know best what *you* need. The Kindle.

The end is important in all things (IV)

Thursday, May 7, 2009

I will end the blog in 30 days.

Another tale from the *Hagakure*:

Once, when Lord Katsushige was hunting at Shiroishi, he shot a large boar. Everyone came running up to see it and said, "Well, well. You have brought down an uncommonly large one!" Suddenly the boar got up and dashed into their midst. All of them fled in confusion, but Nabeshima Matabet drew his sword and finished it off. At that point Lord Katsushige covered his face with his sleeve and said, "It sure is dusty." This was presumably because he did not want to see the spectacle of his flustered men.[28]

Get Rid of Your Excuse (I)

Tuesday, May 12, 2009

In the last two years—the two years of this blog—I have seen artists who claim authenticity copy my work, my website and my sketchbooks. Once a month someone attacks me through my email, usually hiding in the attack his or her shortcomings and lack of integrity—sometimes they go farther and vandalize something.

I have criticized the mainstream art world but my intention has not been to validate bad artists. If things are not happening for you, it's mostly your fault. You might have justifications. If you believe them, it's best to come to peace with what and where you are. If you don't believe them, do something about it.

All artists should assume they have—at best—a tiny talent, and this reality doesn't have to be entirely sad. If you are doing better work today than two years ago then things are looking up.

Stop treading water. Stop diffusing your sadness. Stop being small.

Get rid of your excuse.

Small and Large

Tuesday, May 12, 2009

Thomas cut three mangoes: one for him, one for me and one for his dog, Bill Saroyan, a scraggly mutt who likes all fruits, except apricots. Bill finished first then lay by my side.

"What are you thinking about?" Thomas asked.

"I've been thinking we rarely know the work of an artist in its entirety. We base our ideas on few works without knowing if the effort is small or large," I said.

"What do you mean by small and large?" he asked.

"Many artists dream of having a great retrospective at MOMA but look what it did to Gerhard Richter; few bodies of work benefit from that level of consideration. You see one piece and it seems interesting. You see four and they seem promising. But then you see a hundred and they don't live up to the promise. How many pickled animals should one see before the idea becomes less exciting?" I said.

Bill got up and lay again on a sun patch. He looked comfortable.

"Maybe the oligarch buys the pickled animal precisely because there are other pickled animals in the houses of important people," Thomas said then started to cut another mango.

"Can you imagine Andy Warhol's catalogue raisonné, particularly the pages of the 1980s? Or a vast Kippenberger show? Or seven pieces by Rachel Whiteread? Luckily, demand and dealer savvy scatter the work around the world, sparing collectors the spectacle of 75 camouflage paintings," I said.

"But it's not so simple. The junior-captain of industry who buys the mass-produced thing by Anselm Kiefer or Olafur Eliasson knows he's not buying one of the good ones. And how many people don't know most studies by James Turrell or Christo are merely mementos?" he said.

"They're seeing what's convenient," I said.

"We are all eager to see what's convenient," he said.

Get Rid of Your Excuse (II)

Wednesday, May 13, 2009

As a kid—before moral philosophy and its convolutions—I wanted to understand what lobotomy suggests about happiness. I had seen a Russian movie where someone, after being lobotomized, smiled and got along with everyone. This impressed me. I didn't know anyone who was that happy. Yet, something bothered me about the lobotomy and I spent many hours trying to find what it was. Although, none of the insights I had or have—or have read about—are entirely satisfying, I am certain the answer revolves around the fulfillment of a quality we can call "humanity." This quality is an aim rather than a condition. It is the pearl of the moral/spirit oyster and it might also be an imperative of the species. Humanity is the limit of the spirit, an unreachable reminder of the best we could be, and the *better happiness* moves towards it. This indefensible statement is either self-apparent to you or it is not.

Whatever the case might be, it is clear that humanity is a difficult aim and so, most of us—as Hesse wrote—are half-human and half-worm or half-monkey or half-pig. There are many excuses why we fall short and there are also many internal failures we don't know about. The latter can only be seen through our effect on the world, so they are difficult to resolve. The former—the excuses—are what I want to address here.

Excuses come in many categories, usually manifested in combination: self-loathing ("I'm stupid," "I'm ugly," I'm fat"), victim ("my life is so hard," "the worst happens to me," "I just didn't have the opportunities"), unlucky ("I've the worst luck," "the world dealt me a bad hand"), lone wolf ("I didn't care about that, anyway," "who needs that"), time miser ("I'm too busy," "I did my best," "I tried"), religion ("the meek will inherit the world"), and so on. What all these excuses have in common is laziness. They are ways to avoid doing what needs to be done.

But what do people do with their time if they are not working towards the fulfillment of their humanity? Day to day, they are watching television, dabbling at their work, talking on the phone, feeling sorry for themselves, taking it easy, wasting time. In the long run, they are busy fabricating the lie of why they are not who they could have been. This takes a lot of work but it is the type of work that comes naturally to us. It requires affection for the dressed up game we call "being ourselves," self-satisfaction with our petty choices, and weakness for easy pleasure. Inevitably, while snuggling in that mud pen, we engage in self-loathing, maybe victim and some lone wolf, for good measure (the brutality of self-loathing is not the same as being self-critical with aim towards action.

Self-loathing is self-feeding, being self-critical with aim towards action is life-feeding).

In the case of artists, the excuses apply to their life as well as their art. The problem in both endeavors is the same: it is hard to sustain the imperative of humanity. Most people can get excited to be better by watching a movie, reading a book or having a session of alcohol-induced throw-up. Some can keep that excitement for a week and some for a year, but in the long run, integrity and a higher standard are harder to sustain than it is to fabricate the myth of delightful mediocrity.

If you want to aim higher, the odds are against you. Most likely, you—like me and everyone else—will fail because our tendency is to be superficial and lazy.

A good place to begin is finding people who you admire and who are aiming or have aimed high. Then follow that example by eliminating ideas like, "I am doing the best I can," "I have no time," "I tried." Also, complicate things a little bit for yourself. If, for instance, you find yourself attracted to the model of "the meek will inherit the world," you might want to layer on it the model of the *via crucis*.

Bill Saroyan, Blinky Palermo and The West

Friday, May 15, 2009

Patrice was surprised about Bill Saroyan.

That sweet dog has an interesting lineage. In 1974, Thomas—still a Franciscan and living in New York City—became friends with Blinky Palermo (who deserves a blog entry of his own). One night in the spring of 1975 the two of them were sitting on the stairs of Palermo's building when a very funny dog went by. The West, as they called her, became their dog and when Palermo died she went with Thomas to California. The West is Bill Saroyan's great grandmother.

Stopping the Blog

Tuesday, May 19, 2009

A few people have asked me why I am stopping the blog. I don't have a tidy answer. Nor do I want to pretend it is a big deal. But since even frog tastes like chicken, I will include an excerpt from Ernest Hemingway's Nobel Prize speech as a form of reply; and as an expansion beyond the question also—to where it might want to go.

> Things may not be immediately discernible in what a man writes, and in this sometimes he is fortunate; but eventually they are quite clear and by these and the degree of alchemy that he possesses he will endure or be forgotten.

> Writing, at its best, is a lonely life. Organizations for writers palliate the writer's loneliness but I doubt if they improve his writing. He grows in public stature as he sheds his loneliness and often his work deteriorates. For he does his work alone and if he is a good enough writer he must face eternity, or the lack of it, each day.

> For a true writer each book should be a new beginning where he tries again for something that is beyond attainment. He should always try for something that has never been done or that others have tried and failed. Then sometimes, with great luck, he will succeed.

How simple the writing of literature would be if it were only necessary to write in another way what has been well written. It is because we have had such great writers in the past that a writer is driven far out past where he can go, out to where no one can help him.

I have spoken too long for a writer. A writer should write what he has to say and not speak it. Again I thank you.[29]

The Last Entry

Monday, May 25, 2009

The samurai looks insignificant
beside his armor of black dragon scales.[30]

ENDNOTES

[1] Theodor W. Adorno, "Cultural Criticism and Society," In *Prisms*, Trans. Samuel Weber and Shierry Weber Nicholsen (Cambridge, Massachusetts: The MIT Press, 1983).

[2] Harry Martinson, *The Road* (New York, New York: Reynal & Co, 1955)

[3] Roger Kimball, *Art's Prospect: The Challenge of Tradition in the Age of Celebrity* (Chicago, Illinois: Ivan R. Dee, 2003).

[4] J.M. Coetzee, *Stranger Shores* (New York, New York: Penguin Books, 2002).

[5] Roger Kimball, *Art's Prospect: The Challenge of Tradition in the Age of Celebrity* (Chicago, Illinois: Ivan R. Dee, 2003).

[6] Yamamoto Tsunetomo, *Hagakure: The Book of the Samurai,* trans. William Scott Wilson Tokyo, Japan: Kodansha International Ltd, 2002).

[7] Søren Kierkegaard, *The Present Age of the Difference Between a Genius and an Apostle* (Translated by Alexander Dru. New York, New York: Harper Torchbooks, 1962).

[8] Herman Melville, *Moby-Dick*. (New York: Harper and Brothers, 1851).

[9] Friedrich Nietzsche, *The Birth of Tragedy*, trans. Douglas Smith, (New York, New York: Oxford University Press, 2000).

[10] *Ibid.*

[11] E. M. Forster, *Aspects of the Novel*. (New York, New York: Harcourt, Brace & Co, 1927).

[12] Robert Hughes, "Day of the Dead." The Guardian, September 13, 2008.

[13] Arthur Schopenhauer, *The Wisdom of Life and Counsels and Maxims,* trans. T. Bailey Saunders (Armherst, New York: Prometheus Books, 1995).

[14] Osip Mandelstam, *Modernist Archaist* (Delray Beach, Florida: Whale & Star, 2008).

[15] Søren Kierkegaard, *Fear and Trembling,* trans. Sylvia Walsh and ed. by C. Stephen Evans and Sylvia Walsh (New York, New York: Cambridge University Press, 2006).

[16] Alan Watts, *The Wisdom of Insecurity.* (New York, New York: Pantheon Books, 1951).

[17] Ludwig Wittgenstein, *Philosophical Investigations,* trans. G.E.M. Anscombe (New York, New York: Macmillan, 1953).

[18] Marsden Hartley, "Art and the Personal Life," 1928. http://www.artchive.com/artchive/H/hartley.html (accessed January 9, 2009).

[19] *Ibid.*

[20] Hilma af Klint Foundation. "The Great Commission," http://hem.bredband.net/hilafk/eng/index.html (accessed January 15, 2009).

[21] Yamamoto Tsunetomo, *Hagakure: The Book of the Samurai,* trans. William Scott Wilson Tokyo, Japan: Kodansha International Ltd, 2002).

[22] *Ibid.*

[23] "The loneliness of the Chinese birdwatcher." *The Economist*, Dec 18, 2008.

[24] Statement by G.I. Gurdjieff from *In Search of the Miraculous.* P.D. Ouspensky, *In Search of the Miraculous* (New York: Harcourt, Brace, 1949).

[25] Ludwig Wittgenstein, *Philosophical Investigations,* trans. G.E.M. Anscombe (New York, New York: Macmillan, 1953).

[26] Enrique Martínez Celaya, *Art & the University,* April 7, 2009. Lecture originally presented at the University of Nebraska-Omaha as part of the University of Nebraska Visiting Presidential Professorship.

[27] Joanne Kaufman, "With Kindle, Can You Tell It's Proust?" *New York Times,* April 24, 2009, Fashion & Style section.

[28] Yamamoto Tsunetomo, *Hagakure: The Book of the Samurai,* trans. William Scott Wilson Tokyo, Japan: Kodansha International Ltd, 2002).

[29] Ernest Hemingway, acceptance speech for the Nobel Prize in Literature, 1954.
Ed. Horst Frenz, *Nobel Lectures, Literature 1901-1967,* (Amsterdam: Elsevier Publishing Company, 1969) from http://nobelprize.org/nobel_prizes/literature/laureates/19 54/hemingway-speech.html (accessed May 19, 2009).

[30] Tomas Tranströmer, 2004 "After a Death," trans. Robert Bly (New York, New York: HarperCollins Publishers, 2004).

Disclaimer: This blog was originally intended to promote discussion or contemplation of literary and cultural topics that are typically accessible to the general public. All efforts were made to give appropriate credit to texts referenced in this publication.

First published in softcover in the United States of America by Whale & Star, Delray Beach, Florida
info@whaleandstar.com, www.whaleandstar.com

Design Concept: The people of Whale & Star
Lead Publication Coordinator: Jillian Taylor
Copy: Jason Jeffers, Jillian Taylor, Tessa Blumenberg

Distributed exclusively by University of Nebraska Press
1111 Lincoln Mall
Lincoln, Nebraska 68588-0630
www.unp.unl.edu
Tel: 800/755 1105
Fax: 800/526 2617

Library of Congress Control Number: 2009932945

ISBN: 978-0-9799752-2-6